Build It!

11/00

BUILD IT!

Activities
For Setting
Up Super
Structures

U.S. edition published in 1999 by Lerner Publications Company,
by arrangement with Evans Brothers Limited, London, England.

Lerner Publications Company
A Division of Lerner Publishing Group
241 First Avenue North
Minneapolis, MN 55401

Website address: www.lernerbooks.com

Library of Congress Cataloging-in-Publication Data

Good, Keith.
    Build it! : activities for setting up super structures / by Keith Good.
       p.   cm. — (Design it!)
    Includes index.
    Summary: Presents projects for constructing and testing a variety
 of structures, including bridges, domes, and collapsible structures,
 and encourages readers to design their own.
    ISBN 0-8225-3567-X (lib. bdg. : alk. paper)
    1. Structural engineering—Experiments—Juvenile literature.
 [1. Structural engineering—Experiments. 2. Experiments.]
 I. Title. II. Series.
 TA634.G66 1999
    624.1'078—dc21   99-38339

Printed in Hong Kong
Bound in the United States of America
1 2 3 4 5 6 -OS- 04 03 02 01 00 99

DESIGN IT!

BUILD IT!

**Activities
For Setting
Up Super
Structures**

Keith Good

Lerner Publications Company • Minneapolis

About this book

About this series

This series involves young people in designing and making their own working technology projects, using readily available salvaged or cheap materials. Each project is based on a "recipe" that promotes success and stimulates the reader's own ideas. The "recipes" also provide a good introduction to important technology in everyday life. The projects can be developed to different levels of sophistication according to readers' ability and can reflect their other interests. The series teaches skills and knowledge in a fun way and encourages creative, innovative ideas.

About this book

Understanding structures matters because they are such an important part of our world. Our skeletons are natural structures. So are shells, spiderwebs, and plant stems. People design and make a huge variety of structures to live in, sit on, walk over, carry things, or rely on in other ways. Despite their variety, all structures have to be able to stand up to the forces and loads that they will encounter. Through design projects in this book, young people discover that some shapes are much stronger than others and how this can save resources. Practical activities in this book give an understanding of structures and how materials behave when different forces act on them. Designing stable structures that don't fall over, balancing forces to keep things up, and constructing the main kinds of bridges are also covered through activities. Structures that are rigid but can collapse when we want them to (like baby strollers) are important in everyday life, and this idea is used as a basis for several design projects. Well-designed structures use materials economically. A packaging project raises this issue and encourages wise use of materials. As in every book in this series, the reader is encouraged to get real understanding through marrying "recipes" and knowledge with their own ideas and imagination.

Safety

- A small screwdriver or awl can be used to make holes but the corrugated cardboard must be supported by a slab of modeling clay or thick cardboard – not a hand. Protect work surfaces with a piece of board.

- If a structure is to be tested to destruction (until it gives way), make it from weak materials like the ones suggested in this book, otherwise dangerous amounts of weight may be needed.

- Adult use of craft knives is strongly advised. These must be used with a cutting board or mat and a safety rule with a groove to protect the fingers. Cardboard is often best cut by an adult on a paper cutter with a guarded-wheel cutter.

Contents

Materials and forces
Testing the strength of materials

All designers (including you) need to choose the right materials for their projects. This means knowing about different forces and how materials behave. Structures have to cope with *static* forces like their own weight and *dynamic* forces like wind. When standing on a scale you cause a static force. When you jump on the scale you cause a bigger dynamic force. If we know what kinds of forces will act on a structure it helps us to choose materials that will cope. Paper is very strong when pulled (*tension*) but very weak when twisted (*torsion*). Stone and brick are strongest when being squashed (*compression*) but will not bend without breaking. Try these experiments to find out how some materials behave.

You will need

- strips of paper
- thin cardboard
- 12-inch plastic ruler
- twig
- rubber band
- modeling clay
- string
- piece of fabric

Bending

1. Take a twig and watch closely as you bend it until it breaks. What happened to the top surface? What happened to the bottom surface?

2. Hold strips of paper tightly against the sides of a plastic ruler. Bend the ruler downwards, then upwards. Notice when the strips stretch and squash.

3. Put cuts into both sides of a block of modeling clay and slowly bend it (see illustration below). Which surface is stretched (in tension) and which surface is squashed (in compression)?

Twisting

Try twisting a strip of paper, modeling clay, string, or fabric. Notice how each material behaves.

1 twig

2 paper — 12-inch plastic ruler

3 modeling clay

Stretching

Try stretching modeling clay, a twig, a rubber band, a strip of paper, a piece of fabric, and string. Which resist stretching best? Materials like wire are good at coping with tension.

Squashing

1. Take a twig and push inwards from each end. Is a short twig stiffer than a long one of the same thickness? How do a strip of paper and piece of string or fabric behave?

2. Make a cylinder of modeling clay and compress (squash) it. It is not brittle and won't break, but watch closely how it behaves.

Shearing force

Shearing forces try to make one part of a structure slide past another.

Shearing happens when scissors cut paper or cloth.

1. Use a hole punch, paper strips, and a modeling clay pin to see a shearing force at work. Metal bolts often have to cope with shearing forces.

2. Compare paper strips joined by a paper fastener with strips that have been glued and left to dry. Which is best at coping with a pull?

Making holes for bolts and other parts can cause weakness – this is why many aircraft parts are just glued!

modeling clay pin

paper fastener

glued here

Getting ideas

Design a way to record what happens when you try the activities on these pages. Drawings, charts, lists, and perhaps a computer could help you to show your results. Can you collect other materials to try? Make a poster showing bad or silly uses for different materials, like using cheese to make a ladder, rigid plastic for a tightrope, or string to push something. You could collect and display different materials and pictures of them in use. Think about why different products use different materials. You could separate natural materials like wood and wool from ones made by people, like plastic.

Beams
Making strong shapes

Lots of things that you see every day are shaped to make them strong. Careful shaping saves weight and money, and avoids wasting material. Some food cans and sandwich packages have ridges to make them strong. Why do you think baby strollers are made from tubes instead of solid bars?

A piece of material that has to resist bending is called a beam. The shape of a beam affects how stiff it is and the load it can carry. Here is a chance to find out about beams for yourself.

Some beam shapes to try

You will need

- 8.5" by 11" paper (use scrap paper if you can) cut in half lengthwise
- sticky tape (masking tape is best)
- Weights: standard metal ones, clay blocks of the same weight, or a bag of marbles
- 2 piles of books or another way of making a gap for testing your beams

Tip

A worn-out ball-point pen and a ruler are useful for making creases.

modeling clay

weights in bag

1. Make the beams shown on page 8, using sticky tape to hold the beams in shape.

2. Arrange your books with a gap of 8 inches so that you can test your beams.

3. Try bridging the gap with a flat piece of paper first. Next, test the beams you have made, using enough tape to hold them in shape.

4. Add weight to the middle of your beam a little at a time. **Safety**: Don't use weights that are easily broken or heavy and dangerous!

5. Record the shape of each beam and the weight it carried before collapsing.

Tip

It is sometimes easier to hang weights from the beam rather than trying to balance them on top.

Getting ideas

Try out your own beam ideas. Could you combine some of the shapes to make a new idea? Remember, always start with the same sized paper for a fair test.

Can you think of other ways to support a beam?

Look for strong shapes in buildings, sports and play equipment, and many other things around you. You could record these with notes and drawings.

Strong shapes
Triangles and shells

There are two main kinds of structures. Frame structures are made up from pieces that are joined together. Triangles are rigid shapes, so they are often used to make strong but light frames. You can see triangles at work in construction-site cranes, bridges, bicycle frames, and kites. Shell or *monocoque* structures allow thin material to be made much more rigid by forming it into "shells." Seashells, eggs, and beetle wing covers are examples in the natural world. Domes, egg cartons, plastic bowls, polystyrene food trays, and clear plastic bubble wrap are examples of shell structures made by people. Try making the shapes on these pages and test their strength.

You will need

- strips of corrugated cardboard (the "tubes" in the cardboard should run *along* the strips)
- paper fasteners
- 6 sticks or pieces of wooden dowel rod about 1 foot long
- rubber bands
- white glue
- clear plastic bubble wrap

What to do

1. Make a triangular frame using paper fasteners and strips of corrugated cardboard. Notice how rigid the triangle is.

2. Make a rectangular frame and notice how easily it collapses.

3. Now attach two strips across the frame. This is called *triangulation*. Notice how rigid the structure has become.

4. Remove one of the crosspieces and notice that the frame is still rigid. Part of a structure that can be taken away without weakening it is called a *redundant member*.

5 **tetrahedron**

5. Ask a friend to help you make a *tetrahedron* from sticks and rubber bands (see right). Feel how sturdy it is.

6. Make this bracket from paper fasteners and strips of corrugated cardboard. Glue with white glue. The tubes inside the strips must run along them.

7. Press gently on the bracket and notice how strong it feels.

What to do

Bubble wrap has strong shell structures. The shape makes the wrap much stronger than a flat sheet.

1. Cup your hand over some bubble wrap and press down steadily to feel how strong the structure is.

2. Cut off the flat base to see if this makes any difference to the strength.

To make a special shell structure, see page 20.

6

tie

strut

1

2

The parts of a frame that are being compressed (squashed) are called struts. Parts that are stretched are called ties.

A triangle makes this bracket rigid. The strut becomes a tie when the bracket is turned upside down.

Getting ideas

Think of uses for your tetrahedron. Could it be a shelter, a model of play equipment, or something else? Could a number of these structures be put together to do useful jobs?

Design uses for the bracket you have made. You could make one or two more and use them to support a small shelf. Make the shelf from corrugated cardboard, with the tubes running *along* the shelf.

Collect bubble wrap shell structures. Can you recycle them as covers for hand-held games that you design? Small balls or cut-out shapes could be steered or tapped into parts of the playing surface. The clear shell lets players see but keeps them from touching the pieces.

Stable structures
Testing shapes on a test ramp

It is often very important that structures don't tip over in use. A *stable* structure does not tip over easily. An *unstable* structure will tip over easily. People are not very stable structures. When you stand and lean forward a little you can feel how unstable you are.

The activities here will help you to understand why some things fall over more easily than others. This knowledge should help you design your own stable structures.

You will need

- corrugated cardboard
- thin cardboard
- paper
- masking tape or clear tape
- modeling clay
- drinking straws
- small cardboard box or tube
- cork
- 2 kabob sticks

What to do

Make a test ramp. You can share this with one or more friends.

1. Cut a piece of 8.5" by 11" cardboard in half and join the pieces at the end with tape to make a hinge.

2. Stick a strip of corrugated cardboard across the ramp.

3. Attach some paper to a piece of cardboard. Use modeling clay to make some of the shapes shown.

4. Put your shapes against the strip of cardboard and tilt the ramp very slowly. On the paper, mark the angle at which the shapes topple. Number the shapes and angle lines.

5. Design your own stable and unstable shapes and try them on your ramp. You could also try other objects that won't break.

Do you notice anything about the most stable shapes? Do the least stable shapes have anything in common?

Work out a way to record your results. Show at what angle each shape fell. You could use a computer to help you show your results.

What to do

You might think you can tell how stable a shape is by the way it looks – but you can't always.

1. Tape a modeling clay weight near the top of a small cardboard box or tube. What else could you use as a weight?

2. Test the box or tube on your test ramp. First put the weight at the top, then put it at the bottom. Which way up is the most stable?

Look at cantilevers on page 14.

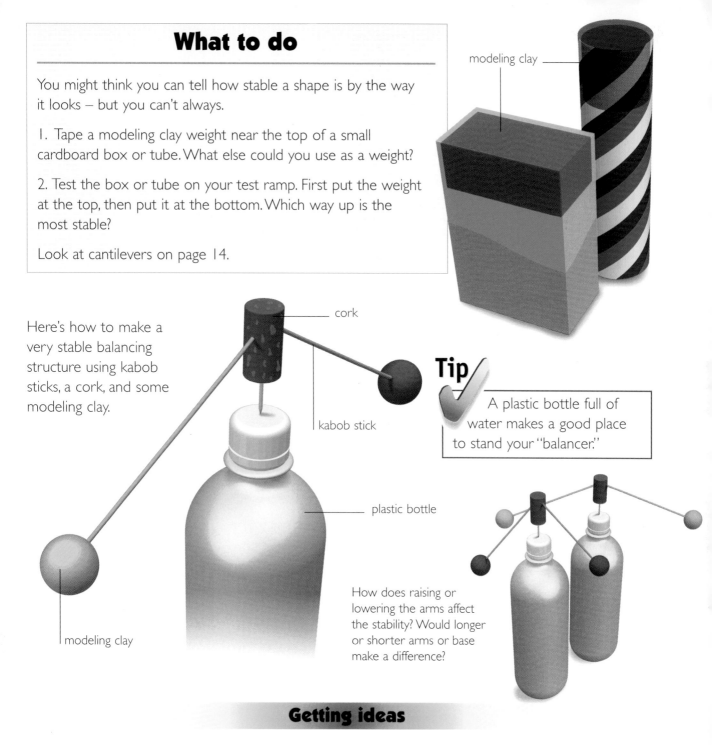

modeling clay

Here's how to make a very stable balancing structure using kabob sticks, a cork, and some modeling clay.

cork

kabob stick

Tip A plastic bottle full of water makes a good place to stand your "balancer."

plastic bottle

modeling clay

How does raising or lowering the arms affect the stability? Would longer or shorter arms or base make a difference?

Getting ideas

Make design drawings for a very stable vehicle that would be difficult to turn over. Make design drawings for a new kind of wheeled vehicle to carry a baby and packages. Could your design carry a toddler too? **Important**: Think about where the weight will go so that your design would not tip over. You could

model your designs, using a construction kit or other materials and clay weights.

Balancer Try using your stable balancer as part of a design for a game. Could you balance things on the balancer? You could word-process a set of rules.

Equilibrium
Balancing forces to keep things up

When two tug-of-war teams pull with the same amount of force they stay still because their pulling forces *balance* or are *in equilibrium*. If two people of the same weight sit on the ends of a see-saw it will balance. Balanced pulling (tension) from different directions can be used to keep things in place. Radio masts, sailing ship masts, metal chimneys, and tents are all held up by balancing the pull of cables or ropes.

Here are some ideas for making structures by balancing forces or getting them in equilibrium. If the forces don't balance, your structures will fall!

What to do

1. Balance a ruler over the edge of a table. Put modeling clay or another small weight on the table end.

2. Put the same amount of weight on the unsupported end of the ruler. How far out can the ruler extend (stick out) without the structure falling?

3. Try adding extra weights to the table end. Each time you add a weight, see how much farther the ruler can extend.

How far can a structure that is balanced in the middle be built out on each side? Structures like this are based on balanced cantilevers – a cantilever is a beam that sticks out from its support. Experiment, using toy wooden blocks.

You will need

- 12-inch ruler
- modeling clay (or small weights)
- rectangular wooden blocks
- paper kitchen towels
- thread
- drinking straw or kabob sticks
- masking tape
- corrugated cardboard
- 8.5" by 11" paper

Making a mast

Using only one sheet of paper and a small amount of masking tape, see how tall a radio mast you can build.

1. Make a base for your mast from a piece of corrugated cardboard.

2. Make stiff shapes from one piece of 8.5" by 11" paper to build your mast (see page 8).

3. Use ties or guy ropes made from thread and fixed with tape to help you support a really tall mast.

Making a tent

Balance the pulling forces on the guy ropes to support tents and shelters.

1. Make a base for your tent from a piece of corrugated cardboard.

2. Try making a tent like the one shown. Use paper towels, straws or kabob sticks, thread, and tape. Make the tent as sturdy as possible.

Getting ideas

Tent structures are used as shelters when fishing or camping, and to keep the sun off. They can also be used to protect explorers and to house people after a disaster. Structures like this are easy to fold down into a small space and are very light to move about. Design and make your own tent structures. You could design a structure with more than one "room." Your structure could be for a special purpose. Think about other structures that could be held up by balanced forces. Could you design a hammock supported by poles and ropes? Look in catalogs to see what other people have designed.

Bridges

Bridging gaps with strength and stability

Bridges are important structures. They make journeys shorter, safer, and easier. Bridges have to be light so that they do not sag under their own weight or waste materials and resources. They have to be as strong as possible so that they can carry heavy loads. There are four basic kinds of bridges: beam, cantilever, arch, and suspension bridges. Find out about bridges by making these.

Beam bridges

Beam bridges can be single span (one beam) or multi-span (several beams).

Frameworks called trusses are often used to make bridges that are strong but light.

cardboard triangles

thin cardboard

The deck of the bridge rests on top of the framework base.

plan

2 inches

2 inches

You will need

- paper straws or dried spaghetti
- thin cardboard and paper
- modeling clay
- corrugated cardboard
- string
- masking tape
- heavy books

What to do

Make your own bridges using straws or sphaghetti to bridge an 8-inch gap, perhaps between a pile of books.

1. Draw the plan on this page full size and build your bridge sides on it. Hold parts still with masking tape while you glue the paper triangles.

2. Turn the frame over carefully and glue triangles on the other side.

3. Let the sides of your bridge dry before joining them to each other. Don't use too much glue, and let it dry well. Glue on a thin cardboard deck (like a roadway) to hold the load.

4. Add a little weight at a time to see how much your bridge can hold. Try different designs and compare yours with others made by friends.

Here are other truss designs. Design your own too. Make full-sized plans.

Cantilever bridges

Cantilever bridges are made up of beams that are only supported at one end. Trap one end of a ruler between heavy books to make a quick cantilever. Often two cantilevers (see page 14) are used with a short beam between them.

Lifting bridges

Lifting bridges are supported at one end so that they can be raised to let ships pass.

modeling clay

What to do

Make a lifting bridge like this from corrugated cardboard.

1. Notice that adding a weight (a *counterweight*) fixed high up makes the bridge very easy to raise. This saves energy and might make it possible for just one person to raise and lower a bridge.

2. Try different amounts of weight. Can you add too much? What would happen if the arch was taller?

Arch bridges

The Romans found that wedge-shaped stones called *voussoirs* could carry heavy loads when built into an arch. Look out for arches in buildings and bridges. Materials that stand up well to compression (squashing), like stone and brick, are used. Modern arches are often made from reinforced concrete. Arches are built over a support that is taken away once the last piece, the middle or keystone, is in place. Strong support is needed at the ends of the arch to keep it from spreading outwards.

1

2

keystone

template

20°

thin cardboard support

What to do

1. Lay thin cardboard between heavy books. Gradually add weights to see how much it can hold.

2. Now make the cardboard into an arch and see how much more weight it will take. Is a high arch stronger or weaker than a low one?

To make an arch that will be strong even though the pieces are not attached:

1. Trace the template below and use it to make an arch out of modeling clay.

2. Cut the arch into the nine voussoirs with a table knife. Build the arch between heavy books on a thin cardboard support.

3. Once the arch is complete, carefully take away the cardboard. Press down gradually to feel how strong an arch can be.

You could go on to try higher and lower arches.

Suspension bridges

Suspension bridges can reach across (or *span*) large distances without using lots of material. In jungle areas they are sometimes made from vines and bamboo. Suspension bridges carrying roads rely on strong steel cables in tension (being pulled). The pulling forces on each cable are in equilibrium; one force is balanced by another (see page 14). Wind can be a danger to suspension bridges, so they have to be designed to cope with it.

deck

tower

direction of tubes

base

What to do

Here is how to make a basic suspension bridge from corrugated cardboard and string. The tubes inside the cardboard must run along the length of each piece.

1. Make the two towers and tape these to a thick cardboard base.

2. Make a deck to reach between the towers.

3. Tie on the strings as shown. Add weight gradually to the center of your bridge to test it.

Look for ways to improve the basic design. How could you stiffen the deck? (See page 8.) Would taller towers make the bridge stronger?

Getting ideas

Find out more about bridges by looking in books and CD-ROMs. Where are there famous bridges, and which is the longest? Make a display about bridges and collect pictures of them. Try to sort them into different kinds, such as beam, cantilever, arch, and suspension bridges. You could add your own bridges and information about your tests. How many stories, songs, or poems about bridges can you find? Perhaps you could write some.

Imagine what would happen if all the bridges vanished. Look at and draw or photograph bridges in your area.

Domes
Exploring rounded shapes

Domes were first built long ago, and they are found in many countries. They vary in shape when seen from the side but they are all circular when seen from above. Domes have been made from clay, wooden poles thatched with palms, fabric, metal, concrete, and even snow. A dome is a kind of shell structure (page 10). A dome can enclose a large space using less material than other structures, and rounded shapes are often stronger than flat ones. If you were to cut a slice from the middle of a dome, you would have made an arch (page 18), which is a strong shape when pressed under weight.

Try making these dome structures to see how strong they can be.

You will need

- plastic bottle
- clear tape
- corrugated cardboard
- round balloon
- newspaper
- flour and water

What to do

1. With adult help, cut the top from a plastic bottle to make a dome.

2. Press down on the top to feel what a strong shape a dome is. Squeeze from the side and the dome feels much weaker.

press down

Tip

If you scoop out the inside of half an orange or grapefruit you have also made a dome.

squeeze

What to do

Make a dome using a balloon as a *form*.

1. Wear an apron and cover your work area with a plastic sheet.

2. Cut a circular hole in a piece of corrugated cardboard to hold the balloon.

3. Blow up the balloon so that it fits snugly in the hole and tie the neck. Support the bottom of the balloon in a box or bowl.

4. Mix flour with a little water to make a creamy paste. Tear strips of newspaper about 1" wide.

5. Brush the strips with the paste, and lay them over the balloon and base. Continue adding strips until you have a layer about 1/8" thick.

6. Leave in a warm place to dry well while you work on the ideas below. When dry, pop the balloon and you have a dome!

Tip A final layer of narrow strips, or even better, tissue paper, will give a smooth finish.

pastry brush

Getting ideas

Your dome could be part of a design for a building of the future, or even part of a city or village of the future. You could model the outside of the building and its surroundings and draw what it is like inside. You could go on to model the inside too. What will the building be for? How could you make your building kind to the environment? Where would the building be built? It could be in a desert, under the sea, or even on another planet. Look at homes from different times, countries, and climates.

Look for domes near where you live or in books and on CD ROMs.

Structures that collapse
Designing structures that fold flat

We can design structures that are strong and rigid but collapse and fold flat when we want them to. This saves a lot of space and makes the products easier to transport. Collapsible structures are all around us; they include folding chairs, ironing boards, tent frames, and camping or picnic furniture. Inflatable water toys, swimming armbands, and even armchairs can be collapsed by letting the air out. Can you think of more things that can be collapsed? Fold-flat furniture allows a room to be cleared for games or dancing. Lots of flattened shelters can fit into one rescue aircraft. Try out some collapsible structures, think of uses for them, and perhaps design your own. Read page 23 for some ideas to help you.

You will need

- corrugated cardboard to make the structures
- brown paper tape or thin cardboard
- thin cardboard or paper

What to do

1. Look at the picture at the bottom. The arrow shows the way the tubes in the corrugated cardboard go. Draw yours out so that the tubes run the same way.

2. Cut the pieces you need from strips that are about 3 inches wide. Mark out the shapes to look like the pictures.

3. Make the creases or joins and put your structures together. To make a sharp crease in the right place, press down on the line with a ruler and lift the corrugated cardboard to bend it.

4. Press gently on your structures from different directions. Do they feel weaker when pressed some ways compared with others?

The slots lock together like this

direction of tubes

Use paper tape or glue thin cardboard

Measure across like this so that the two cross-pieces fit snugly

direction of tubes

Tip

Try out a structure in paper or thin cardboard first if you are not sure how it goes together or if you want to design a new one.

Glue piece 6 on both sides

direction of tubes

Glue pieces 5 and 6 to 1

Getting ideas

Look at the structures you have made. Turn them different ways. What could they be used for? Could they store or hold something? Could you design a gift that would be easy to mail to someone? Could you design games that use the structures? What could go in the holes: pencils, marbles, or something else? You could paint or decorate your finished object. You could design a display stand for one

of your favorite things. Look for fold-flat corrugated cardboard display stands in stores. Imagine that your structures were much bigger and perhaps made from something else. Draw some ideas for using bigger collapsible structures. Ideas could include furniture, survival shelters, or something for the beach. Could you draw fold-flat ideas to help someone who could not find a spare seat on a train?

Pop-ups
Structures that seem to vanish!

Some structures can fold flat then almost put *themselves* up. Children's play tents and tunnels can pop up when taken out of their bag. Life rafts are inflated by gas cylinders, and some life vests blow up automatically when a person falls in the water. Some greeting cards pop up when they are taken out of their envelope. Pop-ups are often used in books to make things look realistic. They are also used in advertising. Try making these structures that pop up when a folded card is opened.

You will need

● thin colored cardboard
● coloring equipment

What to do

To make each pop-up:

1. Cut a piece of cardboard in half. Fold one piece in two to make a base.

2. Draw the *net* of the pop-up carefully on the other piece. Cut the solid lines and score on the dotted ones.

3. Make your pop-ups look like the ones in the pictures. Glue any tabs – but don't use too much.

4. Fold the base card and the pop-up should vanish inside.

2''

0.5''

2.5''

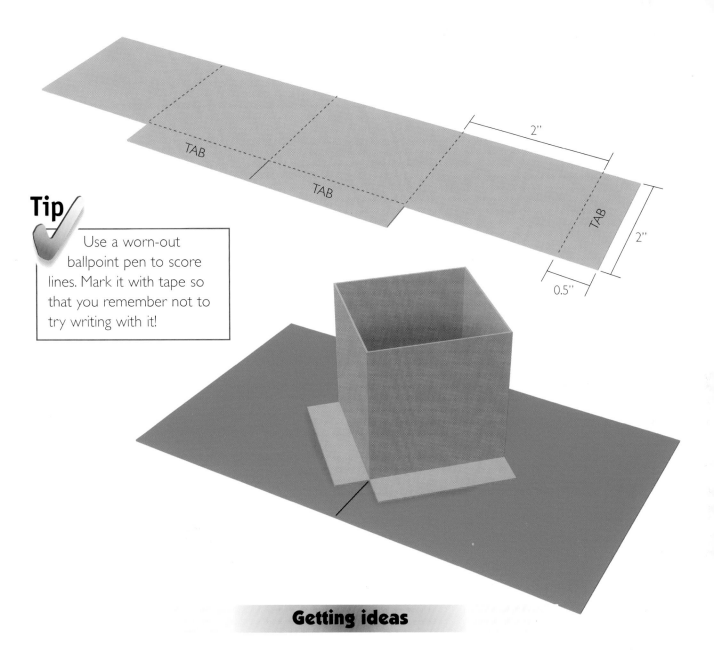

TAB

TAB

TAB

2"

2"

0.5"

Tip

Use a worn-out ballpoint pen to score lines. Mark it with tape so that you remember not to try writing with it!

Getting ideas

What could you use your pop-ups for? Turn the pop-ups and look at them from different angles to get ideas. You could put more than one pop-up on each folding base. Try making your pop-ups into greeting cards or games. Perhaps you could design a greeting card that is also a game! Could game pieces be thrown into a pop-up, rolled at it, or fished out of it? Do holes or slots need to be cut? You also need to think about the age of the user and the kind of rules they could understand.

Use computer word-processing and graphics if you can.

Imagine that your pop-ups were much bigger and draw your ideas. You would need to use corrugated cardboard if you went on to make big pop-ups. What could large pop-ups be used for? Could the last pop-up (above) be used to make furniture or a playhouse if it was big enough? Look for examples of pop-up structures and try to see how they work.

Structures that protect
Designing packaging for fragile objects

Natural structures that give protection include seed cases, nuts, crab shells, and eggshells. Your skull does the important job of protecting your brain. People make structures to protect our bodies, food, and other things. Can you think of things that are packaged to protect them? Protection can be springy like plastic bubble wrap and foam, or rigid like plastic or metal. Protective packaging allows fragile things to be transported or mailed without damage. Like other well-designed structures, a good package uses as little material as possible to do the job. This saves weight and money, and is kind to our environment.

See what super structures you can design to protect fragile objects.

You will need

- thin cardboard
- soda cracker (or other fragile cracker)

What to do

Your design challenge is to protect a fragile object (a cracker) when it is dropped onto a hard surface.

1. Mark out the box as shown on a sheet of thin 8.5" by 11" cardboard. Score on the dotted lines and cut along the solid ones. Cut away the shaded parts.

2. Add any decoration or information to your box (see "Getting ideas") before folding and stapling it into shape. You could use glue, but stapling is quicker.

3. Explore things that could go in your box to protect the cracker (see pages 6–9). Make your protection ideas and fit them in with the cracker.

4. Hold the box closed with a little masking tape so that you can open it easily later.

5. Starting very low, drop the box *bottom down* onto a hard surface like concrete. Drop five times, then check for damage. If the cracker survives, gradually increase the height you drop from.

Safety: You could stand on a chair, but for any greater heights you *must* get adult help.

Tip ✓ Remember, broken crackers are not wasted. They can still be eaten or put in a bird feeder!

shapes that you can try to "protect" your cracker with

Getting ideas

Here are some more things to try. You could just draw your ideas or go on to make and try them. Try protecting the cracker using a range of salvaged materials. Imagine the package is to be mailed – keep it as light as you can to keep the price of postage low. Play around with ideas for delivering the cracker safely. Could a parachute be used, or a slide? Sometimes crazy ideas turn out to be useful. Can you think of other ways to test a package? Could you design something using rubber bands to launch a package against a wall? How could you measure how much force was being used each time? Cars with dummies inside are crash-tested to see how safe they will be for real people. You could draw or model a car that you think would protect the passengers really well. Collect packaging and look at it closely. Packaging is often used to make people want to buy what is inside as well as protecting it, and it may also give instructions. You could design a package like this to help sell a product that you have made up.

Containers

Resisting forces from inside

Natural containers include eggs, nests, seashells, and kangaroos' pouches. People have made containers from many different materials including clay, fabric, glass, wood, cardboard, and steel. Containers are used to hold, store, protect, and carry all sorts of things. Sacks, nets, cans, buckets, and bowls are just a few examples of containers that have to cope with forces from inside.

Thousands of paper bags are used every day to hold and carry things. See if you can design and make a strong, long-lasting, useful, and attractive paper bag. Before you make your finished bag, make a *prototype* to try out your ideas.

You will need

- 11" by 17" paper
- cardboard, string, and plastic that could be used to make bag handles
- corrugated cardboard to make dividers

Crease and fold along dashed lines. Cut along solid lines.

2"

5"

3.5"

5"

3.5"

What to do

1. Follow the pictures to measure, cut, and fold the basic prototype bag. Glue with white glue and leave to dry well.

2. Read the first part of "Getting ideas," then design handles for your bag.

Tip You could use a stapler as well as glue to attach handles.

3. Hang your bag up and gradually load it with weights like oranges or blocks of modeling clay to see how it copes.

You could make more than one bag and try different ideas for handles, or compare your ideas with handles made by your friends.

Once you have made a strong prototype bag that is comfortable to carry, you could use what you have learned to make a finished project. Just one person's idea is shown. What will yours be like?

Think about what will go in your bag. Would carton dividers keep the contents in good condition or make them easier to find?

Tip

It's easier to decorate the bag before it is folded and glued into shape.

Getting ideas

Bags are used for lots of different things. Handles make bags easier to carry. Look at handles on knapsacks, sports bags, carryalls, and others you can find. What could you use to make bag handles that are strong and comfortable? How will you attach them to the bag? Does the bag need to be stronger where handles are attached? How could you do this? Can you make other parts of the bag stronger?

What will your bag be used for? You could add dividers to make different layers. Dessert might be needed last at a picnic and could go on the bottom. Could you make a structure to keep it from being squashed? Would pockets make things easier to find? Does the bag need to be kept closed? How could you do this if it did? You could decorate your bag with paints, perhaps by printing with a carved potato (get adult help) or by sticking things on. Can you think of other ways to improve the basic bag design?

Index